THE GREEK ISLANDS
Genius Loci

View of Naxos island seen through the monumental doorway of the Archaic temple.
Thomas Hope (1769-1831)   Watercolour, 44 x 29 cm.   Benaki Museum, Inv. No. 27375.
© 2010 Benaki Museum, Athens.

Author's acknowledgements

This series of twenty books covering the Aegean Islands is the fruit of many years of solitary dedication to a job difficult to accomplish given the extent of the subject matter and the geography involved. My belief throughout has been that only what is seen with the eyes can trustfully be written about; and to that end I have attempted to walk, ride, drive, climb, sail and swim these Islands in order to inspect everything talked about here. There will be errors in this text inevitably for which, although working in good faith, I alone am responsible. Notwithstanding, I am confident that these are the best, most clearly explanatory and most comprehensive artistic accounts currently available of this vibrant and historically dense corner of the Mediterranean.

Professor Robin Barber, author of the last, general, *Blue Guide to Greece* (based in turn on Stuart Rossiter's masterful text of the 1960s), has been very generous with support and help; and I am also particularly indebted to Charles Arnold for meticulously researched factual data on the Islands and for his support throughout this project. I could not have asked for a more saintly and helpful editor, corrector and indexer than Judy Tither. Efi Stathopoulou, Peter Cocconi, Marc René de Montalembert, Valentina Ivancich, William Forrester and Geoffrey Cox have all given invaluable help; and I owe a large debt of gratitude to John and Jay Rendall for serial hospitality and encouragement. For companionship on many journeys, I would like to thank a number of dear friends: Graziella Seferiades, Ivan Tabares, Matthew Kidd, Martin Leon, my group of Louisianan friends, and my brother Iain— all of whose different reactions to and passions for Greece have been a constant inspiration.

This work is dedicated with admiration and deep affection to Ivan de Jesus Tabares-Valencia who, though a native of the distant Andes mountains, from the start understood the profound spiritual appeal of the Aegean world.

McGILCHRIST'S GREEK ISLANDS

5. PAROS
& ANTIPAROS

GENIUS LOCI PUBLICATIONS
London

McGilchrist's Greek Islands Paros and Antiparos
First edition

Published by Genius Loci Publications
54 Eccleston Road, London W13 0RL

Nigel McGilchrist © 2010
Nigel McGilchrist has asserted his moral rights.

ISBN 978-1-907859-04-5

A CIP catalogue record of this book is available from the British Library.

The author and publisher cannot accept responsibility or liability for
information contained herein, this being in some cases difficult to verify
and subject to change.

Layout and copy-editing by Judy Tither

Cover design by Kate Buckle

Maps and plans by Nick Hill Design

Printed and bound in Great Britain by TJ International Ltd, Padstow, Cornwall

The island maps in this series are based on the cartography of
Terrain Maps
Karneadou 4, 106 75 Athens, Greece
T: +30 210 609 5759, Fx: +30 210 609 5859
terrain@terrainmaps.gr
www.terrainmaps.gr

This book is one of twenty which comprise the complete, detailed
manuscript which the author prepared for the *Blue Guide: Greece,
the Aegean Islands* (2010), and on which the *Blue Guide* was
based. Some of this text therefore appears in the *Blue Guide*.

CONTENTS

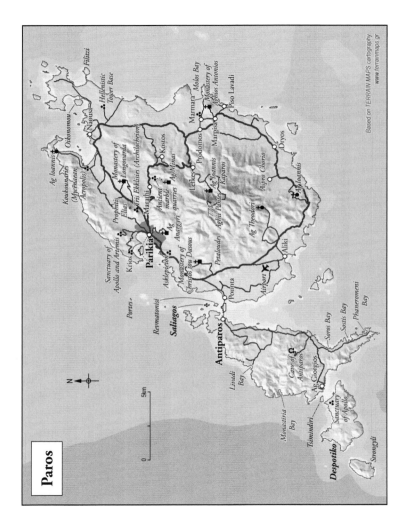

Paros

N

0 5km

Based on TERRAIN MAPS cartography
www.terrainmaps.gr

Filtzi

Oikonomou

Naousa

Helenistic
Tower Base

Ag Ioannis

Koubounaries
(Mycenaean
Acropolis)

Monastery of
Longovarda

Marmara

Monastery of
Ag. Antonios

Piso Lavadi

Molos Bay

Prophitis
Elias

Tris Ekklisies (Archilocheion)

Kostos

Ag Minas

Protonas

Marpisa

Sanctuary of
Apollo and Artemis

Krios

Parikia

Marathi

Ancient
marble
quarries

Lefkes

Ag Ioannis

Kaparos

Dryos

Aspo Chorio

Kalogirnis

Portis

Asklepieion

Ag
Anargyri

Aghii Pantes

Monastery of
Chrissos Tou Dasos

Ag Theodori

Rematonisi

Saliagos

Petaloudes

Pounta

Aliki

Antiparos

Airport

Monastiria
Bay

Livadi
Bay

Cave of
Antiparos

Ag Giorgios

Sotis Bay

Phaneromeni
Bay

Soros Bay

Tsimindiri

Despotiko

Sanctuary
of Apollo

Strongli

PAROS

Paros produces what is considered traditionally to be the best quality of marble for sculpture in the world. If it had been more available to him Michelangelo would surely have used it. Many of the greatest sculptures of Antiquity, from the *korai* of the Athenian acropolis to the *Hermes* of Praxiteles, are in Parian marble and they derive much of their appeal from the material itself—its responsiveness to the tool, its brilliance, and its translucence above all. In 1844 the ancient quarries were opened again specifically to furnish the stone for Napoleon's funeral chamber at Les Invalides. Much of the early economy of Paros was based on the exploitation of its marble, and of the sculptural expertise which it fostered. The island became prosperous and full of outward-looking initiative as a result. In the 7th century BC it founded a very successful colony on Thasos, whose veins of gold and silver made Paros even richer. On board the ships that set out from Paros to colonise Thasos was the greatest individual the island has given birth to—the 7th century BC poet Archilochus—whom the ancients viewed as almost as great as Homer himself. No-one better than he expresses the spirit of those early times: the restless energy of the Greek imagination and the new-found freedom of the individual. Archilochus is

the island-poet *par excellence*—a distillation of the independence of mind and the uncluttered horizons which
are the particular preserve of the island world.

In 326 St Helen, the mother of Constantine the Great,
found herself on Paros. With her customary generosity she
was inspired to found a church on the island. She vowed
to build it and then continued on her way to Jerusalem,
where she was to die. It was probably built by her son in
the end and it is the earliest church in the Aegean which is
still in constant use today. Paros wears its greatness lightly.
It is only small, but it has three beautiful towns—Parikiá,
Náousa and Léfkes—of quite different and contrasting
characters. On the island it is possible to eat well, visit remarkable monuments and bathe on some of the most attractive beaches of the Cyclades. Ten minutes away is the
island of Antiparos, with a famous and impressive cave
in whose vast halls of stalactites the Marquis of Nointel
stage-managed a full celebration of mass with music and
fireworks on Christmas Day in 1673. Then, beyond Antiparos, is the deserted island of Despotikó, Ancient *Prepesinthos*. There is a ferment of archaeology on the Parian
islands in general, but the most interesting site currently
being revealed is here on Despotikó, untouched by any
later habitation. It is a sanctuary of the Archaic era probably dedicated to Apollo, of which only a fraction has so

far been uncovered, but which may prove to be one of the most significant recent finds of the Cyclades.

HISTORY

Paros and its outlying islands have a rich prehistoric archaeology, which begins with the settlement on Saliagos dating from the 5th millennium BC and continues into Early Bronze Age culture, whose cemeteries and settlements from all around the island have yielded valuable material revealing commercial contacts with other Aegean islands, Crete and the Greek mainland. An important settlement at Koukounariés dates from the last years of the Mycenaean period; after its destruction in the 12th century BC the site was re-inhabited and seems to have prospered during the Geometric era. The island was colonised by Ionians and in the 7th century BC established its own colony on Thasos—an expedition in which one of the greatest poets of early Greek literature, Archilochus, participated. Thasos brought her mother-city great wealth, and Paros enjoyed its golden age of influence and creativity in the early 6th century BC when many of its finest buildings were raised and the quarries of its preeminent marble were first seriously exploited. By the end of the 6th century BC the island was under the dominion of Naxos. In 490 BC Paros sent a trireme with the invading Persian fleet, an action which brought upon it a retaliatory attack by Athens, under Miltiades, after the Battle of Marathon. The islanders resisted in ingenious ways (Herodotus, *Hist.* VI, 133), and during the siege Miltiades broke his knee in the Sanctuary of Demeter. The siege was lifted: Miltiades returned to Athens in disgrace and the injury to his knee which had turned gangrenous eventually took his life. Paros did not contribute to the defeat of Xerxes in 480 BC, and afterwards became subject to Athens. During the Peloponnesian War it tried to shake off Athenian dominion, failed, and was assessed to pay the highest tribute of any Cycladic island, namely 18 talents annually. Free for a brief period after 403 BC, it was then incorporated in the second Athenian League in 377 BC and came under Macedonian influence after 357 BC. From 100 BC, Paros was part of the Roman Eparchy of Asia. Both Agorakritos in the 5th, and Scopas in the 4th century BC, were sculptors from Paros: Scopas was one of the greatest of his age, and worked on the Mausoleum of Halicarnassus. The visit in 326 AD of St Helen, mother of Constantine the Great, resulted in the building on Paros of one of the most important churches in the Aegean, the Panaghia Katapolianí, often called '*Hekaton-*

tapylianí or 'Church of a Hundred Gates'. Justinian rebuilt
the church more grandly in the 6th century, probably after
a fire had destroyed the original Constantinian structure.

As a favoured base for Saracens and pirates during
the 8th and 9th centuries, the island became poorer and
dramatically less populated. Its fortunes revived when it
was taken by Marco Sanudo in 1207 into the Duchy of
Naxos; in 1260 the Kastro was built in Parikiá. In the 15th
century the capital was moved to the castle on the hill of
Kephala on the east coast of the island, which was believed
to be easier to defend against the increasing pressure of
Turkish attacks. In 1537 Khaireddin Barbarossa laid siege
to the castle and captured it in four days. The island was
thereafter to remain under Turkish dominion, with an ad-
ministrative centre at Léfkes, for almost 300 years. Piracy
once again flourished, and Hugues Creveliers, the original
of Byron's *Corsair*, was one of the many celebrated pirates
who operated from Paros in the 17th century. During the
Russo-Turkish War of 1768–74 Náousa became the naval
base for the Russian Aegean fleet of Count Alexei Orloff.
Paros was re-united with the fledgling Greek State in 1832,
at which time it became the home of the heroine of Greek
Independence, Mando Mavrogenous (1796–1840): she is

buried in the courtyard of the Katapolianí church in Parikiá.

The approaches to the harbour of Paros are notoriously hazardous, and it was on the isolated reefs called the *Portes* at the entrance to the Bay of Parikiá that the ferry, *Express Samina* from Piraeus, foundered in a storm on the 26 September 2000 with the loss of 80 lives.

The guide to Paros and its outlying islands has been divided into four sections:
- *Parikiá and its immediate vicinity*
- *Náousa and the north of the island*
- *Léfkes and the central-southern loop*
- *The islands of Antiparos and Despotikó*

PARIKIA AND ITS IMMEDIATE VICINITY

The island's capital of Parikiá, built over the city of Ancient *Paros*, spreads on the east side of a wide bay, protected by a hook of land which curves round to the north of it. In antiquity some of the hill-tops ranged around were crowned with sanctuaries and temples; today whitewashed monasteries and churches have taken their place. The focus of the city, then as now, was a low hill by the shore just south of the port, from where habitation spread east into the shallow, fertile valley inland which possessed good water below the surface, accessible through wells. Ancient *Paros* was a particularly rich city—assessed by Athens to pay a tithe of 18 talents, proportionate to its wealth, into the treasury of the Delian League: this was bigger than any other Cycladic island and more than that paid by its prosperous neighbour and competitor in all things, Naxos, who at most paid only 15 talents. Modern **Parikiá** also has an air of prosperity. Even though not as stunningly sited as some, it is still one of the loveliest towns in the Cyclades for the charm of its streets and the quality of its life. Two contiguous main streets traverse the length of the town: running north/south, inland of the hill of *kastro*, is Market Street, often just referred to as '***Agorá***'; the northern extension of this,

Grávari Street, turns east from below the Kastro and goes as far as the church of the Panaghia Katapolianí, which marks the edge of the old town. Since this church is the island's most significant monument, we begin with it, followed by the important Archaeological Museum which lies just to its east.

THE CHURCH OF THE KATAPOLIANI OR 'HEKATONTAPYLIANI'

See detailed plan of the church on page 95.

The **church of the Panaghia Katapolianí*** (or **Hekaton-tapylianí**) is the oldest and the most historically important church in the Aegean Islands (*open daily 8–1 & 4–9*). In spite of the damage wrought by Khaireddin Barbarossa in 1537 and by several earthquakes—especially in 1773—the church has survived as an active place of worship for nearly 1,700 years, something that cannot be said of many other places in the Christian world. Today it has predominantly the appearance given it by the architect of the Emperor Justinian in the 6th century; but by the time he took the building in hand there had already been a church and baptistery (still visible) here for 200 years, built over a pagan structure. It is an extraordinary sensation to find a building of such Constantinopolitan grandeur in the Cyclades. The building was substantially cleaned, consolidated and purged of later additions in the 1960s by the veteran Greek archaeologist, Anastasios Orlandos.

The history and development of the complex

Baptisteries—as places of symbolic death and re-birth—were frequently built on or near the site of a martyrdom: this was a way of celebrating the death of a martyr by acknowledging his or her rebirth into a new life beyond death, as well as reinforcing the intercession of the martyr on behalf of the neophytes subsequently baptised on the spot. The cruciform baptistery here to the south of the main church, which is possibly the oldest element of the complex, may have come into being shortly after Constantine's edict of tolerance in 313 in order to commemorate the martyrdom during the persecutions of an unknown figure on this site in the ancient city's *gymnasium*. Like many other vulnerable sites of martyrdom and baptism, this could have been lost and forgotten, particularly in the Dark Age of the Saracen invasions of the 8th century. But the fortuitous visit of St Helen, the pious mother of the Emperor Constantine the Great, who quite probably put in at Paros during a storm, as tradition relates, on her way to Jerusalem in 326–7, brought the building suddenly to the forefront of the Christian con-

sciousness. In gratitude for a safe onward journey to the
Holy Land, St Helen vowed to build a church to the Virgin on
the site beside the baptistery. She was a generous benefactor
of new buildings wherever she went. Helen died in 328, but
her wishes must have been fulfilled after her death, perhaps
on the orders of her son, so that the baptistery was enlarged
and a timber-roofed, basilica church was built to its north in
c. 330 AD i.e. around the time that the city of Constantinople
was being re-founded. The building had, like Constantine's
basilicas in Rome, a large, porticoed atrium in front with a
central fountain—a feature which functioned for ablutions,
just as in Islamic mosques today. The 4th century chapel of
St Nicholas in the northeast of the existing church, which
had a different dedication at that time (St Nicholas lived in
Asia Minor in the 4th century and his cult became common
only much later) may also predate the visit of St Helen, like
the Baptistery; or it may have been a part of the Constantinian basilica built after her death. We cannot say for certain.

The reasons why, 200 years later in the 6th century under the Emperor Justinian, the whole church was rebuilt
in a new form with a vaulted roof and dome, are less clear.
Justinian in his long reign strove to bring a new unity to a
deeply divided Church and to give the Empire new impetus
and identity through an ambitious programme of building.
The 4th century, Constantinian church may have been de-

stroyed by fire, and its rebuilding may have seemed a good opportunity to assert an imperial presence at the very heart of the island communities. According to tradition, one of the two architects Justinian had employed for Santa Sophia in Constantinople—probably Isidorus of Miletus—was sent to Paros to superintend the new building which was to be executed by a pupil of his named Ignatius. The Katapolianí has many architectural characteristics in common with Justinian's churches in Constantinople—especially with Aghia Irini which was built in 536 AD.

As you visit the buildings, it is important to bear in mind the chronology: 1) the **monastery buildings** enclosing the church and courtyard were added in the 17th century; 2) the main **church of the Virgin** and its portico, or narthex, date from the 6th century; 3) the smaller church now incorporated into the northeast corner of the latter, the **chapel of St Nicholas**, and the **Baptistery** to the south of the complex, both date from the first half of the 4th century AD; 4) the whole ensemble is built over a 4th century BC **Gymnasium** of the ancient city.

The name

The church, dedicated to the Dormition of the Virgin, is referred to by two names, both of which are first recorded in written sources in the 16th century. '*Katapolianí*' refers to the site of the church which is *kata* ('across from' or 'down from') the *polis* (city), i.e. not in the city, but slightly outside of it; and '*Hekatontapyliani*' is a typically periphrastic, Byzantine compliment to the beauty of the church, which symbolically possessed *hekaton* (one hundred) *pyli* (gates). The first name might have be used for Constantine's original church of the 4th century, the second, for Justinian's later rebuilding; but both names have survived and are commonly used.

The main (6th century) church of the Panaghia

As you approach the church, the three-arched entrance (*tribelon*) to the narthex is echoed by a three arched window above (belonging to the gallery of the church) and yet another three-arched window in a pediment above that. Apart from the pleasing architectural rhythm of this, it gives an intimation of how luminous the interior will be. The building is preceded by a spacious, transverse portico, supported by ancient architrave beams which function as the vertical supports here, filled at ground level with 7th century marble closure panels. The plan of the interior is a centrally domed cross of unequal arms, c 40m in length and 25m in width—spacious but not overwhelming. The dome, vaults and floor were rebuilt in the restoration of the 1960s. The windows—strongly reminiscent of the churches of Constantinople—may originally have had marble frames, with panes of thin, translucent Parian marble, which would have imparted a softer, glowing luminosity to the interior. In front of the eastern piers of the dome, a couple of modern glass panels in the floor reveal two columns from the buildings of the **ancient Gymnasium** at the lower level beneath both standing on well-preserved marble bases. The iconostasis is a composition of different elements: the screen includes an **ancient frieze**, which runs the entire width at about chest height; the columns in different marbles, carved in heavy relief with vines, are also ancient pieces with 7th century carving; the rest of the screen all dates from the 17th century, in a grey Tiniot marble, which strikes a melancholy note here by comparison with the more joyous, white, Parian marble of the island. The **icons**—mostly covered with protective silver revetment—were the gift of the of the Mavrogenis family (*see pp. 34–36*) in the 18th century. The only uncovered icon is the beautiful *Dormition of the Virgin* to the right, a fine Cretan work of the 17th century. Against the northwest pier is a venerable icon of the *Praying Virgin*, dated to around the year 1200.

The spaciousness of the interior is greatly enhanced by the **Women's Gallery**, or *gynaecaeum*, which runs around the interior at the upper level—another decidedly Constantinopolitan feature of the church: it beautifully articulates the interior space, together with the arcade of columns and capitals which supports it. Only a few of its closure panels are original; most are modern replacements. The gallery is entered by the flight of steps outside the church in the southwest corner; it provides the best views of the interior and of the area of the sanctuary behind the templon screen. The sanctuary is spacious: the liturgical drama takes place in front of an impressive **synthronon** (seven rows of seats), below a central episcopal throne flanked by two lesser seats, and centres on an altar covered by the ribbed dome of a magnificent **ciborium**, made originally from a single block of marble, supported on four antique columns. Beneath the altar table is an *aghiasma*, or natural pool of sacred water. This would have been the water used in the adjacent baptistery. The **paintings** on the wall above date from the early 17th century: they illustrate the stanzas of the *Acathist Hymn* to the Virgin—a sacred hymn to the Mother of God which originated in the 6th century. Their surface has been regularly chipped in preparation for the application of another layer of plaster and painting on top; the surface chipping would help the new plaster 'key into' the existing layer. The painted seraphim visible in the pendentives of the main dome (an unusual iconography, shared by Santa Sophia in Constantinople) are of the same period

In a recess of the north wall is the small chapel or **oratory of the Blessed Theoktiste**, built around her tomb in the floor. She was a young nun from Methymna on Lesbos in the 9th century; she was captured there by pirates, but escaped on Paros when the boat carrying her into captivity stopped on the island. She took refuge in the church of the Katapolianí, lived and eventually died there as a hermit after 35 years. She is a patron saint of the island.

The (4th century) chapel of St Nicholas

The chapel of St Nicholas, more a small church in its own right, which fits snugly into the northeast shoulder of the main church, still has an air of great antiquity imparted by its solemn rows of **fluted Doric columns** which were taken from a pagan structure and converted into a church here during the reign of Constantine. Justinian replaced the original 4th century pitched, timber roof with a vault and central dome, which was restored in the last century. In the sanctuary are a small *synthronon* and throne again and vestiges of *opus sectile* **floor** to the south. At the east end of the north wall of the chapel, the remains of **murals** of St Elizabeth and her son, St John the Baptist, date from the 7th/8th century; whereas the painting of Christ and the Apostles in the conch of the apse is from a thousand years later.

The Baptistery

The broad proportions and gentle light make the Baptistery a space of great beauty. It is contiguous with the main church and connected by a door directly into its south side. This is probably the oldest element of the complex, predating St Helen's visit and, as one of the oldest surviving baptisteries of Christendom, is comparable in antiquity and state of preservation with the baptistery of St John in Lateran, in Rome. Once again, the original 4th century construction was in the form of a timber-roofed basilica with an apse, and once again it was given a dome and vaulted roof by Justinian in the 6th century. It is entered through three doors whose frames are all constructed of ancient marble architectural elements. The **cruciform font*** for baptism by immersion, created from carved slabs of antique Parian marble, may belong to the original phase of the building. The idea that the officiating priest balanced stylite-like on its central column, as some have suggested, is surely erroneous: the neophyte passed from west to east via the steps, with the priest standing to one side. Small areas of the 6th century coloured, **mosaic floor** with abstract designs are visible at three points (just north of the west door, beside the north door into the main church, and just southwest of the font). The only surviving area of wall-painting, figuring *St George and an Angel,* dates from the 12th century. There are many ancient *spolia*: above the west door is a fine **frieze of egg-and-dart design**, with dentils above, taken from a Hellenistic building. In the southwest corner are stacked fragments of the original *ambo* from the Constantinian church (with vine and peacock designs), and the broken segment of the *ciborium* dome (with curved ridges).

The whole complex of buildings is visually bound together in a simple and pleasing fashion by a projecting, dimpled cornice which runs round the interior of all three buildings and unites them.

The courtyard

The courtyard in front of the main church, filled with flowering trees and cypresses, occupies the area of the porticoed atrium of the first Constantinian structure. Today the monastic buildings which surround it are all from the 17th century. The central area is like a museum of ancient fragments and *spolia*—Early Christian and pagan. The southwest corner is occupied by a small **Ecclesiastical Museum** (*hours as on p.14*), containing a good collection of **icons**. Most date from the 17th and 18th centuries, but the earlier exhibits are of particular note: a fine 16th century icon of the *Crucifixion*, and the painted sections of the **15th century sacristy doors***, depicting the *Apostles, Peter* and *Paul* and an *Annunciation* scene. There is also a beautifully carved, wooden *epitaphios* of the 18th century.

Along the north wing of the courtyard, you will notice a curious **monumental gate** in a classical revival style. Dating from 1678, this was once the monumental doorway of the church. The columns which frame the door stand on squat marble bases sculpted into grotesque, pot-bellied, mustachioed figures, similar in style to those in the portico of *Agora Street*, just below the Kastro.

To the north and east of the Katapolianí stretches a grove of dense pine-trees, contrasting refreshingly with the white buildings all around and recalling how the island— certainly up until Roman times, if not beyond—was once densely wooded. To the south side of the church is the High School, above which can be seen an interesting row of late **Hellenistic and Roman sarcophagi** with successive funerary panels of different dimensions carved into their front and sides. These were receptacles of composite family burials, which were carved with new, individual panels honouring the dead, as successive burials were added. They mark the entrance to the **Archaeological Museum*** of Paros (*open daily 8.30–3.30, except Mon*), a small collection with some exceptionally fine sculptural pieces. Given the preeminence of both the island's marble and the renown of its schools of sculpture, this collection is of particular importance: even the smallest and most fragmentary pieces are of sophisticated workmanship, and nothing should be skipped for what it potentially reveals about the methods of master stone-cutters. The museum spreads across a main building with two wings, a portico in front, and an outside courtyard.

In the centre of the courtyard is the early 4th century BC **floor mosaic** found beneath the church of the Katapolianí, which depicts the *Labours of Hercules*, a typical subject for a *gymnasium*. It is colourful and clear in design: the **head of the lion** which composes part of the frame is particularly well executed. In the open air area, is a wide variety of funerary furniture—cinerary urns, carved *stelai*, and *cippi*—altars, and architectural elements in local marble. A row of **sarcophagi shaped in human form** from the Archaic period on the south side of the court are unusual finds, presumably of Near Eastern influence. The best-conserved, carved *stelai* are displayed under cover along the north side of the court, together with an Early Archaic, **giant Cycladic pithos** with impressed design, at the far right-hand end.

Ahead, under the portico, stands the twice-life-size, **cult statue of Artemis** from the temple at the Delion (*see pp. 49–50*) north of Parikiá, recomposed from over 40 fragments. At the end of the portico to left, is the elegant, late 6th century BC, **Ionic capital*** which bears a 4th century BC **dedicatory inscription to the Parian poet Archilochus** (*see pp. 46–49*), and which may have formed the central memorial inside a heroön dedicated to his memory: it would probably have stood on top of a column and been surmounted by a sphynx, in the centre of a temple-like mausoleum, which was preceded by two altars. The inscription attests that it was a certain 'Dokimos, son of Neokreon, [who] dedicated the piece as a votive offering at the tomb of Archilochus of Paros, son of Telesikles'. Beside it, against the walls, are exhibited the densely-inscribed plaques in Parian marble which relate to incidents in the life of the poet, and other subjects. The other superbly carved, 5th century BC architectural elements on display—especially the **lion's-head spouts and the foliate frieze of the *sima*** (*front wall*) from the upper portion of a Classical building–come originally from Delos, but were found immured in the walls at the Katapolianí.

Room 1 (*ahead and left*) contains prehistoric and early material from Paros. The earliest piece is the Neolithic figurine of the 4th millennium BC from Saliagos (*see pp. 74–75*) of a steatopygous female commonly referred to as the '**Fat Lady of Saliago**' (*first case to left*), who is a close cousin in form and conception of the figurines of fertility goddesses and 'Fat Ladies' found in Malta, which date from the same era. In the same case are a couple of examples of large picks made from blocks of obsidian from Milos, used for rough-shaping larger marble objects such as bowls and cups, before the finer work and sanding down began. Opposite is a very fine **8th century BC amphora, decorated with a battle-scene***: of particular note is the central figure who carries a figure-of eight shield, of the kind used by Homeric heroes. Mounted warriors, dead hoplites and grazing horned animals compose a curious battle-landscape of the mind. Also of particular interest (*left wall*) is a remarkably early **grave stele of the 7th century bc**, delicately engraved with a very faint image of a seated woman on a decorated throne. Amongst the exhibits from later epochs are two **miniature three-legged tables in marble** (*case at back left of room*) which were 4th century BC offerings at the sanctuary of Delian Apollo: they give us a rare glimpse of Hellenistic furniture. On exhibition in the room (*rear partition*) is the inscribed marble panel known as the **Parian Chronicle***, the greater part of which is in the Ashmolean Museum in Oxford (a cast of which is also displayed): the Chronicle was drawn up in

c. 264/3 BC in the archonship of Diognetos, and is a dated record of historical events in the Greek world and of important Greek writers, since the time of King Kekrops of Athens in the mid 2nd millennium BC. Its importance in helping verify Greek chronology has been considerable. Two beautiful fragments from Parian marble **Archaic *korai***, one wearing an exquisitely defined and decorated chiton, stand at the centre of the room.

Room 2 *(small room in the middle)* exhibits objects from the excavations on the island of Despotikó, to the south of Antiparos. These include the painted, cult **figurine of a female deity** in terracotta *(central case)*, dating from the early 7th century BC, wearing a crown over highly stylised hair and a clearly defined, almost naturalistic, face. Opposite *(to the left on entering)* are three beautifully carved, heads of Archaic *kouroi* of quite distinct and different styles. In the cases around the walls are votive objects which attest to the wide-ranging contacts which the Sanctuary of Apollo had: these include a considerable number of bronze items.

Room 3 *(to the right)* is dedicated to Archaic and Classical marble sculpture. Of particular importance are: the **winged marble figure of Gorgon*** *(first bay)*, who, in her capacity as a powerful apotropaic image who turned away evil, was placed on the tip of a temple pediment as if just alighting. In one hand she clutches the head of a snake which encircles her waist: half woman, half flying monster, her innate ugliness has been transformed by the artist's skill into a beautiful and dynamic sculpture—a flowing unity of soft and well-proportioned volumes. The work dates from the mid 6th century BC. From 50–60 years later are two exceptionally fine late Archaic pieces: the lower portion of a relief of a standing **female figure wearing a pleated chiton** (*on right in doorway to second bay*); and the statue of an **enthroned goddess***—probably Artemis—remarkable for the very fine rhythmic flows and counterpoints of the pleated drapery. On the reverse side of the partition behind the latter is a marble **relief of the poet Archilochus** reclining on a dining-couch, faced by his wife, and surrounded by his emblems as both a warrior and a poet: this and the adjacent panel of a hunting scene (both of which had been latterly immured into the courtyard walls of the Katapolianí) constituted part of the frieze of the monument dedicated to the poet, and date from c. 500 BC. Virtually no painting, other than vase-design, exists form the Classical period: it is a fortune therefore that the mid-5th century, **marble disc, painted with the figure of a discus thrower*** in cinnabar (*right wall*) has survived. It is a unique piece, found in the burial of an athlete. Beside it are two 6th century, ***kouros* fragments** which show how the sensitive medium of Parian marble is particularly adapted to the delicate description of the subtly varying volumes of the human body. Similarly, in the *Nike* (c. 470 BC) which stands in the centre at the end of the gallery (*third bay*), the stone effortlessly takes on the lightness of the fall of drapery in its beautifully counterpointed movement. Of particular note are the two fragments of the upper parts of grave *stelai*, one depicting a young woman's head, the other a young man's, both of the 5th century BC: the workmanship is unostentatious, sensitive and perfect in both. It is this combination of lightness and sensual detail which is the particular quality of the ancient Parian school of sculptors.

CHURCHES AND STREETS OF PARIKIA, BELOW THE KASTRO

Just to the south of the front entrance of the Katapolianí is a large ruined building standing in an area of walled garden, referred to as the '*Frangomonastiro*', or Frankish Monastery—in reality the remains of what was the *catholicon* of the **monastery of the Capuchins**, built in 1700 but shortly after destroyed during the first Russo-Turkish War in 1770—standing next to the Roman Catholic church of St Anthony.

The area to the west, between the church of the Katapolianí and Kastro, traversed by **Grávari Street**, is an attractive network of streets with mostly low Cycladic houses of two floors, often with trellised courtyards and wooden balconies on the upper floor, which extend over the street in places creating small covered passageways. The external corners of buildings are frequently rounded to facilitate the passing of loaded donkeys and mules. Along the main thoroughfares are a number of prominent neoclassical façades of houses built by prosperous merchant families. A number of these can be seen towards the western end of Grávari Street. A good example is the coloured and pedimented façade of the **Demetrakopoulos Mansion** (*south side*). The house has a walled court to one side, a central balcony in wrought-iron supported on carved marble volutes, and a coloured trabeation which is attractively dentillated. It was built in the first decade of the 20th century.

The majority of the churches in the lower part of Paros date from the 17th century, a period of renewed prosperity, stability and relative commercial freedom for the island: they mostly do not have wall-painting, but have carved wooden iconostases, paved marble floors, and, in some cases, the traditional Cycladic raftered ceiling of reed-wattle covered with a layer of seaweed and bound and sealed in a 'cement' made with sand and crushed seashells. Of the many churches, three in the lower area of the town stand out.

To the north side of Grávari Street is the church of the **Panaghia Septemvrianí**, built in 1592, set back behind a paved space with trees and a supine, fluted ancient column. The door is framed with a marble surround and the interior embellished by a finely carved marble iconostasis. Inside, the design is simple and dignified, with unusual spaciousness given by a wide narthex. Two ancient Doric capitals are incorporated into the corners between the narthex and the *naos*, and a third constitutes the altar: other *spolia* peek out from the plaster. Fifty metres further west, and one block to the south on Karavia Street, is the church of the **Presentation of the Virgin (Eisodia tis Theotokou)** of 1645, in which the dome is built on arches supported by marble columns and capitals: in the vault over the altar are some damaged wall-paintings of the 18th century. One hundred metres further south of here, in the area of Tholákia, is the church of **Aghia Marina** (1623), just off Odos Skopa on what is referred to as the '*Nea Odos*'. In the area are several 17th century churches—Aghios Artemios, Aghios Ioannis, Aghii Anargyri—but Aghia Marina is the most interesting of all, recognisable from outside by the incorporation of two beautiful fragments of ancient decorative cornice, one of which functions as a window-ledge. Inside are many more *spolia*—ancient column fragments and upturned capitals—as well as a fine 17th century **sarcophagus front** opposite the door of entry. The marble templon screen displays a particularly beautiful **icon** of the *Virgin and Child*, of the 16th century.

At the point where Grávari and Agora streets meet is a substantial municipal building with an arcaded porch, supported on a couple of slender marble columns, which probably dates from the late 16th century. To either side of the arcade are two crudely carved reliefs of **grotesque figures**—a man (*right*) and a woman (*left*) apparently holding their stomachs. They appear to originate from the same fantasy, though less well-executed, as the two contorted figures below the pillars of the removed 17th door-

frame (*see p. 23–24*) of the Katopolianí complex. Below
the female figure, a piece of marble with an antique inscription has been incorporated upside down. Opposite is
a carved marble **water-fountain**, one of three in the town
(here, at Panaghia Septemvrianí, and at Aghia Triada), all
dated 1777 and all the gift of the Paros-born dragoman,
Nikolaos Mavrogenis, who built the aqueduct that fed
them with spring water. From the fountain, a street leads
uphill to the Kastro, whose walls made from hundreds of
ancient *spolia* and fragments are glimpsed ahead.

THE MAVROGENIS FAMILY OF PAROS

The Mavrogenis were a Phanariote family—that is,
they were 'old' Greeks from Constantinople who had
lived in the area of *Phanari* (today's *Fener*) on the
Golden Horn. When the city was captured by the
Turks in 1453, a part of the family stayed; others left
for the Peloponnese, from where they later moved
to Paros in 1715. They were educated and wealthy
people; Petros Mavrogenis served as combined British and Austrian consul in the Cyclades, and he sent
his son Nicholas (b. 1738) to study in Constantinople with relatives who were '*dragomans*'—respected
translator-envoys for Ottoman affairs in the pay of

the Sultan. Nicholas followed a similar career and, as a brilliant linguist and a favourite of the Grand Vizier, Yusuf Pasha, he rose fast in the hierarchy and was eventually honoured with the title of 'Prince of Wallachia' (Romania). He staged an ostentatious entry into Bucharest followed by a coronation in May of 1786, and appears to have run a wayward and extravagant court in the city: his horse was given the honour of having the bedroom next to his own in the palace. But Mavrogenis was not without many redeeming features: from the start he insisted that the peasantry should be able to make their appeals to him directly and in person, and he constructed a gazebo specially for such audiences. His legislation helped both the Jewish and Orthodox communities, and he did much to help and protect his native Cycladic islands. On Paros, the aqueduct and marble fountains of Parikiá and the lavishly cased icons are the most visible testimony; but he also restored churches, built schools and upgraded the port facilities.

At first successful in his military campaigns, Mavrogenis ultimately failed the Ottoman cause when the Habsburg army invaded Wallachia in July 1789. A second defeat in 1790, cost him his life: he was killed on the Sultan's orders and his head was sent to Istanbul to be impaled at Top Kapı. His remains were later buried in Bursa. Thomas Hope, who knew Mavrogenis personally, included aspects of him in his remarkable novel, *Anastasius*, which took London by storm when it appeared in 1819. It is an irony that the grand-daughter of this prince of the Ottoman Empire should have been Mando Mavrogenous, the heroine of the Greek Revolution against Turkish rule. Mando died on Paros in 1840 and is buried in the courtyard of the Katapolianí.

KASTRO

The northern side of the hill of Kastro was occupied in prehistory by a settlement of the 3rd and 2nd millennia BC. Later, from the 6th century BC onwards, the eminence was the site of the **sanctuary of Athena** (*?Poliouchos*, or 'Protector of the City'). This included an imposingly large temple put up when Paros was under the domination of Naxos and its tyrant Lygdamis, in the 520s BC. Its construction is contemporary, therefore, with the unfinished structure of the 'Portara' on Naxos; in fact deductions made from the measurements of fragments incorporated into the walls of the Venetian castle now built on its site, indicate that it may have had a door-way commensurate with the Portara. The hill has substantially eroded on its western side due to seismic activity, and two thirds of the temple lies buried under the sea below. The remains that are visible, in and under the church of Aghios Konstantinos, represent only its eastern extremity (the front), before which would have stood the altar. The marble temple was an Ionic-style building, with two six-column porticos to either end (i.e. *amphiprostyle*), supporting an undecorated trabeation, pediments and a pitched roof.

Climbing up to the Kastro from the waterfront, you come immediately to the stacked rows of drafted gneiss slabs which constituted the platform of the temple: the temple itself was constructed of white Parian marble, which contrasted with the green-grey schist of the podium. Inside the church of **Aghios Konstantinos** (entered through the adjacent church of the Evangelístria to the south), several courses of the lateral **walls of the temple's cella**, in rectangular marble blocks, can be seen constituting the lower part of the north wall. Over the church's carved west door-frame is a cross made from Iznik tiles: only the upper arm of the cross is of antique (16th century) tiles, the others are modern reproductions. The adjoining 18th century church of the **Evangelístria** (Annunciation) has a low **arcaded porch** on its southern side, supported by Early Christian window elements coming from the Basilica at Tris Ekklesies (*see pp. 45–46*). In the street which curves northwards from the church, ancient *spolia* are so abundant that column drums are used as tables in the porches of houses.

On the left side of this street, rise the walls of the **Venetian castle**, built around 1260 by Angelo and Marco (II) Sanudo. A good half of the castle has suffered the erosion of the west side of the hill and has finished in the sea together with the temple of Athena, leaving the northeast corner as the best preserved sector. It is constructed from hundreds of marble blocks, architraves and columns obtained by demolishing temples and other ancient structures on the site. The phenomenon is common all over the Mediterranean, but the scale of it here is breathtaking: it is hard—even if ingenuous—to imagine that the elimination of what must have been majestic, if ruined, marble temples and their conversion into masonry for a fortress with such a paucity of architectural quality to it, did not give the 13th century builders some twinge of regret. The walls are nonetheless a fascinating mosaic of ancient pieces; in which long rows of column drums on their sides, alternate with courses of rectangular blocks, incorporating 5m-long elements of the **temple's marble portal**: at other points there are (partial) **inscriptions** on blocks and elements of **decorated cornice**. The marble is Parian, but comes from areas of the quarries where it is delicately veined with grey. This was 'constructional grade' marble, as opposed to the pure white which was of 'sculptural grade'. Apart from the material from the temple of Athena, elements were also taken from an Archaic temple of Persephone and Kore within the ancient city (according to Gottfried Gruben), from a long Doric stoa of the Hellenistic period, and possibly from the temple of Demeter outside the city which is mentioned by Herodotus (VI, 134). One curiosity, visible from the south, high up at the top of the northeast bastion, is a round, 4th century BC, tower-like structure or *tholos*, originally dedicated to Hestia, goddess of the hearth: its shape served as a ready-made apse for the **church of Christos** which was built around it, high up inside the bastion. The church was partially removed by archaeologists a century ago, so as to reveal the ancient structure.

From below, it is possible to see the overall curve in the walls which gave the fortress a slightly elliptical form. The four churches in the northeast corner, from south to north are: the Panaghia tou Stavrou, built in 1514, Aghia

Ekaterini, Aghios Ioannis and the chapel of Evangelístria (1752). Between Aghia Ekaterini and Aghios Ioannis, the southeastern wall of the latter is 'buttressed' on the out-side by a fluted column lying at its base and covered in countless layers of whitewash.

SOUTH OF PARIKIA

At the southern end of the promenade, the shore-side road rises towards a windmill and makes a detour round the small, cuboid chapel of **Aghia Anna** (*key in house op-posite Demarcheion, 50m to south*), which is almost en-tirely constructed from ancient blocks of Parian marble. Originally a 17th century chapel, it was restored in 1900, and then re-pointed with a mortar made with marble dust after an accidental fire in 2003. Two hundred metres further west, just beyond where the shore road rejoins the peripheral road, a scarp rises to the left (south) where there are the vestigial remains of two places of cult—the Hellenistic **sanctuary of Asklepios** on the lower terrace just above the road, and the Archaic sanctuary of **Apollo Pithios** (his father) on the level above. Of the latter little remains, except some of the retaining terrace and parts of foundations. A small memorial chapel, built as a pastiche of a Hellenistic mausoleum, marks the site. More has sur-

vived from the 4th century BC **Asklepieion** below, which
occupies a site typical for such a place, beside some rising
springs of mineral water (now almost dry) and situated a
little way out of the inhabited centre—two elements essential for the treatment and the isolation respectively of
the sick who frequented the place. The sanctuary centred
on a Doric '*abaton*' or cultic building, projecting per-
pendicularly from a stoa which ran along the base of the
scarp. The rectangular, **marble-lined pools** by the springs
can be seen against the rock.

EAST SIDE OF PARIKIA

At the junctions and on the ring-road to the east of Parikiá is a plethora of brown signs indicating minor archaeological sites, wherever excavation has taken place.
The size of the sign often does not correspond to the importance or interest of the site. The most significant are
the following:

Archaic ceramic workshop (*just west of the peripheral road,
two blocks in, and to the south of the main car-park, underneath the extension of an apartment building to the left of the
street*). The workshop comprises two large **kilns**, constructed
in packed masonry, several smaller kilns, and two lined tanks

for preparing clay, one of which has a mosaic floor. Potsherds from the site indicate that the workshop was in use through the Classical and Hellenistic periods. 200m to the north, a comparable sculpture workshop, with unfinished, small-scale sculptures in it, has also been uncovered.

Hellenistic/Roman house (*underneath the 'Pensione Evangelitsa', north west of the main car-park on the west side of the peripheral road: access down steps into basement*). Both the steps to the original upper floor and the imposing marble door-posts and threshold can be seen; a curiosity is the small earthenware pot set into the window shelf. The house dates from the 2nd century BC.

Hellenistic houses and the walls of the ancient city (*east of the peripheral road, from the junction just south of the Archaeology Museum*). The foundations of several Hellenistic, residential blocks have been uncovered in the area immediately east of the peripheral road: several fine, non-figurative floor **mosaics** have been revealed and are visible in situ. The large lozenge shaped design surrounded by a 'running wave' frame is of beautiful colour, which can be revived with water. Under one corner where the mosaic is missing is visible another, older layer beneath in a different and earlier technique. Further up the road, above the modern cemetery, a section of the **Archaic walls**, built of large blocks of schist, is visible; the monolithic door-jambs of a **gateway** have also survived.

The Aghios Panteleimon area (*behind the building across the main road and adjacent gulley, from the upper, eastern tip of the pine-grove beside the Katapolianí*). This is a large area— part cemetery, part sanctuary—which has yielded a number of important pieces of sculpture, including the *Gorgon acroterion* and two *kouroi*, now in the Archaeological Museum. The finding of the *Gorgon* suggests that there may have been an, as yet unidentified, Archaic sanctuary here. The most visible remains are of the stepped, **circular, Archaic funerary monument** in white marble, which bears the incisions in its top for the fixing of a dedicatory column or votive statue. Clearly visible on its first and second steps are several **antique 'graffiti'** incised into the marble: these include names, the image of a house, a phallic symbol, and many footprints. The latter, which are found widely on Paros, were a common way for visitors to pay their respects to the commemorated hero or athlete, and to leave their mark.

The ancient cemeteries (*beside the post office, just in from the waterfront, 200m east of the church of Aghios Nikolaos*). This is one of the richest cemeteries excavated in the Cyclades so far, whose range of interest and importance comes from its having been continually used from the 8th century BC until the late Roman period. It was remarkably well organised, with walls dividing it into areas according to family or clan. Many different kinds of burial practice are represented: there are **8th century *polyandria***, or stone-lined compartments for group or multiple burials, containing cremated ashes in amphorae; early cist graves for inhumations; graves made of ceramic tiles; Hellenistic **marble urns** with marble lids for ashes; and, most visible of all, the Roman-period **sarcophagi**, with lids designed as pitched roofs, and sides decorated with funeral banquet scenes. Several **standing, marble, grave *stelai*** can be seen in the area, standing on stepped bases: the tallest one visible was a boundary marker for the Geometric cemetery; the two smaller ones close to it, mark individual graves of the Classical period. A small **exhibition space** at the edge of the area displays a variety of marble burial urns, and the skeleton of a horse which was buried presumably with its owner as a grave offering.

The first turn east from the peripheral road south of the museum climbs steeply up to the **monastery of the Aghii Anargyri** (2.5km), which overlooks the whole area of Parikiá and its bay from the east (*open daily 10–2, 4–sunset*). The monastery is built in front of a tiny grotto with a seeping spring of fresh water (south chapel), which may have functioned as a hermitage in earliest times. Although the existing buildings date from the mid-17th century, the monastery is said to have been founded by a refugee who left Constantinople before the city fell to the Turks in 1453.

A kilometre and a half east of Parikiá, beside the main road to Náousa, is the possible location of the **Heroön of Archilochus**, or *Archilocheion*, at a site known today as 'Tris Ekklisies' ('three churches'), named after the three 17th century chapels which formerly stood here, which were removed by archaeologists when the site was fully explored. The chapels were built over the remains of a large **Early Christian basilica** of the 6th century whose broad, three-aisle plan with apse is now clearly visible, as well as the foundations of an unusual apsidal chapel which obtruded from the middle of the south wall. The large threshold blocks in the west with door-locking slots and the fixtures for the feet of the ciborium can be seen. The **paving of the sanctuary** in Parian marble is of particular fineness, and many **columns, panels, capitals** and **templon elements** in the same brilliant material have been set up at various points across the site. These pieces were nearly all taken from pagan buildings and reused or re-cut; this explains why such a high proportion of them bear Hellenistic inscriptions, and why several of the blocks show the **incised, ancient imprints of feet**—one in the floor of the central nave; others just to the south. There is a marked number of these intriguing and beautiful symbols on Paros (*see circular monument at Aghios Panteleimon, p. 43*), which elsewhere are most frequently found in sanctuaries of Isis and Serapis as votive gifts or records of the presence of devotees of a cult. In the 1950s the inscribed plaques, now in the museum, referring to the building of a heroön to Archilochus, in response to an utterance of the Delphic Oracle, were found not far from here; and when Tris Ekklisies was excavated shortly after, the 6th century BC Ionic capital with the dedicatory inscription to Archilochus, also in the museum, was found on the site. It is therefore generally believed that Tris Ekklisies marks the site of the original monument to the poet; and that the blocks incised with footprints may have belonged originally to it.

ARCHILOCHUS

Archilochus is the other side of the Greek literary medallion from Homer. He lived in the mid 7th century BC and was therefore writing more than one hundred years after Homer. His subjects are not heroic but human; his metre not monumental, but flexible and profoundly mimetic of speech; his stance not elevated but involved, witty, passionate, bitter, erotic, funny and self-ironic by turns. In the metaphor that he himself coined—'the fox knows many things; the hedgehog knows one great thing'—he was the archetypal, multi-facetted fox. He presents for the reader his own constantly changing moods and experiences of living. He writes the earliest love-lyric lines in Greek, is often seen as the father of satire, and had a profound formal influence on Horace. Reading him today still gives unexpected pleasure.

Like some Renaissance *condottiere*, Archilochus was both poet and professional soldier. He was possibly the bastard son of an aristocratic Parian family, and accompanied his father, Telesikles, on the crucial mission from Paros to colonise the island of Thasos. He lived there unhappily for a while—perhaps to get away from his native island where he had been bitterly disappointed: a certain Lycambes who had promised his daughter, Neobule, to Archilochus in marriage, later withdrew his consent, drawing the sharpest satire of early literature upon his head and that of his offspring. Its effect was said ultimately to have destroyed them. But Archilochus is certainly not all bitterness or anger: his honesty and his self-awareness are always life-enhancing. Though an effective soldier, in one battle against a Thracian tribe he threw away his shield and fled the battle-field: in no way ashamed of his action, he commemorates its realism instead and comments wryly that he could easily get himself another shield anyway. He relates the incident with ironic humour in a way that heralds the coming of age of a new Greek humanism. His verse celebrates a pugnacious freedom and individualism. He was killed around 652 BC, in a battle against Naxian forces, by a certain Calondas, called 'Corax', 'the crow'. The oracle of Apollo at Delphi cursed Calondas for having slain a favourite both of Apollo and of the Muses.

The sensitivity and nervous energy of his writings (which have come down to us in only fragmentary form) are inseparable from the formal metre in which they are written. The invention of short flexible units of *iambic trimeters* and *trochaic tetrameters*, and the loose arrangement of the epode as a structure, gave his verse the agility to change mood as quickly as the weather. Archilochus's greatness was never in doubt throughout Antiquity, and it is revealing of the Greek temperament that he was revered almost as much as Homer was; hence the elaborate *heroön* here on Paros, where the poet's cult could be perpetuated. The monument was said to be the haunt of hornets and wasps.

NORTH OF PARIKIA

On the panoramic summit of a rocky spur, 3.5km by road north of Parikiá, are the remains of the **sanctuary of Apollo and Artemis**, known also just as the 'Delion'— built on a site which shows evidence of cult since prehistoric times. The eminence has unimpeded views in every direction: west to Siphnos, east to Naxos, and—crucially for cultic reasons—north to Delos. The *peribolos* of the area is traceable: it is square in outline, with the temple situated in the southwest corner, oriented on an east/ west axis, and with the altar visible to the east. A short distance to the south is a separate structure, which possessed marble benches and a portico, which appears to have been an **ancillary building**, and could even have been a *hestiatorion* or feasting room. The temple possesses a deep recess beneath the floor-level of the interior, which probably functioned as the treasury for votive gifts; against the west wall would have stood the cult-statue—the colossal figure of Artemis, whose form has been re-assembled from countless fragments, and stands in the portico of the Archaeological Museum. The fragmentari-ness of the ruins and the small size of the broken pieces lying around suggest that the temple and statue suffered deliberate destruction. The choice of materials is interest-ing: the construction is partly in granite and partly in dif-fering qualities of local marble. What has survived of the **threshold** is in very finely cut, purest Parian marble. The masonry would indicate a date in the early 5th century BC. There is an extraordinarily dense scatter of potsherds, with fragments of painted pottery visible in places, and even minute pieces of necklace and bronze still to be seen on the surface.

If instead of branching for the Delion, you follow the road from **Livadia** all the way to the west, at 2.5km from Pariká a left turn leads down to **Krios**, where set back from the shore is a curious building dating probably from the Late Roman or early Christian period. It stands to an impressive height of 6m, is over 20m in length, and is char-acterised by a hemicycle at its east end which is the width (8.5m) of the whole building. There are no columns, aisles, windows or stone furniture which would suggest it were a place of worship, even though it is oriented precisely on an east/west axis. At about 3m from the ground, a ledge of Parian marble divides the height of the hemicycle: these marble pieces have been identified as seats taken from the 4th century BC *bouleuterion* of Paros. This use of *spolia* and the method of construction point to a date in the Late Roman/Early Christian period. The proximity to a protected shore and the large windowless space is similar to the so-called *tholoi* on Kalymnos, Agathonisi and Pharmakonisi in the Dodecanese, which are thought to have functioned as magazines and storage places. The 'apse' here may simply be a way of countering the thrust of the hillside into which the building is deeply cut.

Beyond Krios, the road finishes at the point of the headland at the church of Aghios Phokás (5km). The west side of this barren and rocky promontory is perforated with large caves and grottos; the one furthest south is dubbed the 'Cave of Archilochus'.

NAOUSA
AND THE NORTH OF THE ISLAND

(Parikiá = 0.00 km for distances in text)

THE NORTHWEST

Along the route from Parikiá northeast to Náousa are several places of interest beside the way. At 3km, after passing Tris Ekklisies, the steep hill of **Prophitis Elias** rises 261m to the west of the road. It was the site of several places of cult in Antiquity. The summit is best reached from the western side of the hill (*left turn at 3.5km, round north side of hill*) up a track which passes a picturesque, abandoned monastery.

The chapel of Prophitis Elias sits on the summit where once, according to an inscription found on the site, was the cult of Zeus *Hypat[i]os* ('the Highest'). Down the spur to the southwest, at a point overlooking the port below, is a plateau with a raised knob of rock about 3m x 1m, which may correspond to the **altar of Aphrodite** or of **Eileithyia**, divine protectress of childbirth, whose cults are also attested here: nearby are a couple of shaped blocks of limestone which must have been part of the structure, and some cuts in the native rock lower down. Continuing west to the edge of the spur, you come to a cave in the rock with **votive niches**; nearby are rocks with— once again—the faint outlines of feet incised on them, left behind as votive acts by women who frequented the shrine.

On the slope across the valley, to the east of the main road (*turnings at 2.5km and 3.7km*) stands the **monastery of Longovarda**, dedicated to the Zoödochos Pigi ('Fount of Life'), and built on the site of a fresh-water spring, now dry, in a ravine in the hills (*open to male visitors only, 9.30–12*).

The buildings of the complex have grown substantially over the years since it was founded, or rather was moved from Náousa, in 1638. It was almost immediately rebuilt and enlarged in 1657 in a form commensurate with its new status as a *stavropegic* monastery (i.e. under the direct administration of the Ecumenical Patriarchate of Constantinople). The interior of the domed, 'free-cross' *catholicon* is entirely decorated with (now darkened) murals. The upper areas—pendentives, drum and cupola—are the original 17th century work, while large areas lower down were repainted in the 19th century. Of particular note are two small icons executed by two brothers who were monks, Hierotheus and Methodius, painter and wood-carver respectively, in the late 19th century. The right-hand icon is meticulously and minutely carved with scenes of the Life of Christ—a piece of rare and extraordinary skill. At the end of the 19th century the monastery counted 125 monks: there are now nine.

As the road descends to **Plastirás Bay** the landscape changes dramatically: the limestone promontory to the northwest has a convoluted and knotty form, of a kind familiar from Delos, Mykonos and parts of Tinos; the bay is dotted with small islets; and the impermeable bedrock has created a wide alluvial plain behind the shore. It is a configuration and marine landscape that seems to have appealed to Neolithic man, and it is no surprise to find that one of the most important Neolithic cemeteries of the Cyclades was excavated here, and that the bay has given its name, as a result, to a stylistic genre of Cycladic sculpture. The 'Plastiras group' of Cycladic figurines are perhaps the most distinct and recognisable of all—less schematic and more naturalistic than other types, with stocky bodies, clearer facial features, often very elongated necks, and sometimes an unusual headgear on the heads of the male figurines. Of the excavated Neolithic cemetery little is to be seen; but of its Bronze Age successor on the hill of **Koukounariés**, there are clear remains. The **Mycenaean acropolis** is on the knob of hill immediately west of the westernmost point of Plastirás Bay (*2km to the west of the main Parikiá/Náousa road, shortly before it enters Náousa: ascent of the hill is from the southwest side*).

The site overlooks the whole bay below, the plain behind, and the channel between Naxos and Paros: a protective ravine encircles it to north. A lower enceinte of fortification walls in large polygonal blocks can be seen in places. Just short of the summit is a wall running east/west constructed in large, oblong mansonry, enclosing a flat area above, which is traversed by the foundations and bases of interconnected buildings of large proportions, as well as of smaller dwellings. In the store-rooms, just inside the main wall, were found bronze weaponry, vases and domestic items, as well as stores of stone projectiles—all buried in ash, indicating a destruction by fire in the late 12th century BC. Curiously, what was built here was also begun in the 12th century BC; so the existence of the settlement in Mycenaean times was short. It continued to be inhabited after the destruction until the 7th century BC, after which time it was deserted. Fifty metres southeast of the summit is a hollow whose floor is cut by archaeologists' assay trenches; to the south of these can be seen the remains of dwellings and the base of a temple (probably dedicated to Athena) dating from the Geometric period.

From Koukounaries, the road continues a further 3km
to an isthmus where there are boatyards and a couple of
protected beaches, overlooked by the picturesque monas-
tery-church of **Aghios Ioannis**, just short of the northern
tip of the island. In the marshy streams south of Koukounaries, the night-heron (*Nycticorax nycticorax*) can
sometimes be seen by day: it returns each year from its
winters in the Nile Valley to breed by the coast here.

NAOUSA

Náousa* is a beautiful series of contiguous harbours,
backed by a small and attractive Late Mediaeval town. It
is given unusual character by a stream of fresh water—the
Elytas stream of Antiquity, according to some authori-
ties—which comes from near Matzoro in the hills to the
south and runs down a channel in one of the streets of
the town into the sea. Náousa has grown considerably
in recent years owing to its understandable popularity
as a tourist destination. Although the wider area of the
Bay of Náousa is dotted with prehistoric and Geometric
settlements and Hellenistic installations, the town itself
does not appear to have a significant ancient precursor
even though antique *spolia* are seen all around the historic centre. The moles of the central **harbour** were first

constructed in the early 16th century, when a small **Venetian fortress**, in the form of a tower, was built to mark their outer extremity. This now constitutes the heart of the existing castle, which appears to have been enlarged in the next century by the addition of a circular structure all around, perforated with artillery embrasures just above the water level. It is similar in concept and date to the Venetian fort at Avlemonas on Kythera. During the Russo-Turkish War of 1768–74 the Bay of Náousa was the Aegean base for the Russian Navy. Today the intimate inner harbour and the delightful buildings which encircle it are home to a colourful fleet of fishing caïques.

Woven into the tight Cycladic fabric of the old town are several 17th and 18th century churches. The most interesting of these is the church of **Aghios Ioannis Theologos** (1629) in the centre of the original settlement. A small narthex gives onto a wide, domed interior, without any lateral arms, which was once entirely covered with idiosyncratic **wall-paintings**. The murals are signed as the work of 'the Sakellarios [Giorgios] Mostratos' and dated 1784: a '*sakellarios*' is an ecclesiastical treasurer or *sacellarius*. The north wall is dominated by a *Last Judgement*, precisely drawn and meticulously compartmentalised into pictorial vignettes. In the apse is the customary '*cosmic hierarchy*' in which the Word descends from the Almighty, passes through Christ, and down to a painted ciborium behind the real altar, with painted bible and chalice in position. This is not great painting, but the overall effect, presided over by a fine *Pantocrator* in the dome, is not unpleasing. A particularly beautiful 17th century **icon of St John the Theologian** with Prochorus, to the right of the doors of the templon, is worthy of note. Many of the churches of the town display typical, **open-latticework belfries** in local marble. Beside the church of the Ypapanti (the Purification of the Virgin), uphill a short way to the southeast, rises an abundant **spring** of slightly brackish water, which also flows through the streets.

Across the fresh-watercourse, on the west side, is the former monastery of **Aghios Athanasios** which is now a small **Museum of Byzantine Art** (*open daily 9–3 except Mon, Easter–mid-Oct*), worth visiting alone for the small series of **salvaged wall-paintings*** which have been brought here from the rural church of Protoria, near Náousa. They are the oldest surviving Byzantine paintings on the island, and their intensity and simplicity, combined with their decorative vocabulary suggest a date in the 12th or 13th century. One of the fragments depicts the donor praying. The collection also displays **icons** of the 17th and 18th centuries, including works by the local Mostratos brothers.

THE NORTHEAST

Two kilometres east of Náousa is the base of a cylindrical **Hellenistic tower** (*reached by two successive first-left branches off the main road after it turns south to Marpisa*). Known locally as '*Palaiopyrgos*', the tower stands to almost 2m in height, with four courses of regular 4th century BC, trapezoidal masonry which are well preserved. The position has not been chosen for strategic surveying of the coast or sea routes, and its purpose on a low eminence in the middle of an open fertile area must have been related to the protection of the surrounding agricultural land and activity. To the southeast are the foundations of a wall of the same period, suggesting that the tower may have been the centre of a farmstead. To the south, a plain of grain fields, dotted with oaks, stretches as far as the twin Kephalos hills which sweep to conical summits above the coast. To the north, the beetling promontory of Viglákia has subsided in recent geological history, leaving its irregular shape surrounded by detached islets. A prehistoric settlement, clearly surrounded by a wall, is still visible on the **islet of Oikonomou** to the west of the neck of the peninsula, while at **Filitzi island** on the eastern side there are the ruins of another ancient settlement.

LEFKES AND THE CENTRAL AND SOUTHERN LOOP

(Parikiá = 0.00 km for distances in text)

THE ANCIENT MARBLE QUARRIES

The source of Paros's superb marble lies 5km due east of Parikiá along the road to Léfkes, in a valley which cuts south from the eastern end of the settlement of **Maráthi**. The whole area has much evidence of 19th century quarrying activity. The shell of a large **marble-cutting factory** stands on the southwest side of the valley: it is a particularly fine relict of industrial architecture, with a low triangular profile, arched windows and oval window-light in the pediment. These buildings date from shortly after the reopening of the quarries on Paros in 1844, for the specific aim of providing marble for the tomb of Napoleon at Les Invalides. In 1878 the *Société des Marbres de Paros* was created to exploit the quarries further.

Three hundred metres south of the road, in the eastern slope, opposite two ruined 19th century buildings which originally housed hauling machinery, are the entrances to the principal **galleries of the ancient quarries***, active since the early Archaic period. (*Flashlight and sturdy footwear are necessary to explore the galleries.*)

The two galleries, whose entrances you see before you, descend over 100m into the hillside and communicate at their farthest point by a transverse gallery which permits an essential movement of air. They descend at the same gradient, but diverge from the parallel in their trajectories. A series of smaller chambers and galleries radiate from the extremity of the northern gallery. The steepness of the gradient must have doubled the difficulty of extracting large blocks. Small debris was left to accumulate on the floor of the gallery and this facilitated the movement of cut blocks over its surface. But from the outset the gradient must have been dictated by the purity of the particular vein of marble, which must follow the angle indicated by the slope of the natural roof over the entrance to the south gallery. A descending gallery in this way also allows for the escape of smoke and fumes from the burning of lamps.

Of the two galleries, the southern is more interesting, but more difficult to descend. The **northern gallery** has been worked in the 19th century, and the drill marks along the walls, and the supporting walls date from this recent period: whereas in the **southern gallery** (to the right as you face the hill) can be seen evidence of ancient working—the fine and regular striations left by ancient picks and bull-nose chisels—

in the roof and along the walls. On the left as you enter the south gallery, carved into the rock-face behind a protruding boulder, is the mid 4th century BC, ***relief and inscription dedicated to the Nymphs**, protectresses of these 'artificial caves'. The scene—fragmentary and eroded by superficial efflorescences—in fact depicts nymphs, satyrs, silens, and other figures (possibly Pan) whose identity is hard to decipher: the three-word inscription is so elliptic that its meaning is also far from clear. The subject matter of the scene may relate in some way to the legend recounted by Pliny that in the quarry on one occasion, when the stone-breakers split open a block 'a likeness of Silenus was found inside' (*Nat. Hist.*, XXXVI, 14). As you descend the gallery, on the right there are regularly-spaced, natural columns of rock left so as to give support to the roof. At various points there are graffiti left by visitors from the 18th century onwards. At the bottom of the two galleries the space opens out: it appears that the greatest quantity of marble was extracted from here.

Two hundred metres further up on the west side the valley, quite high on the slope, is a natural breach which was quarried superficially in Antiquity; and a further 100m beyond is another deep quarry, which progresses into the hillside in a series of chambers. A few unfinished blocks can be seen around its entrance. In these two areas the marble is less pure and is slightly veined with grey.

PARIUM MARMOR

No marble in antiquity found greater favour with the sculptor's craft than Parian marble: it is the white marble *par excellence*. It excels even Naxiot marble in both transparency and in the fineness of its crystalline structure. Whiter marbles such as Carrara marble—*marmor Lunense* as the Romans called it—have since been used and were the staples of Michelangelo, Bernini and Canova; but they do not approach Parian in warmth and softness. The quarries on Paros in fact produce more than one kind of marble: the most valued quality was referred to as '*lychnites*', from λύχνος, a lamp. According to Pliny (*Nat. Hist.*, XXXVI, 14) and Varro, this was because it was 'quarried by the light of oil lamps'. Hesychius, on the other hand, said the name referred to the celebrated translucence of the marble which could transmit the glow of an oil lamp. It is *lychnites* which was extracted in the underground galleries here at Maráthi. But it could be obtained only in smaller blocks, large enough for most sculpture, but not in the quantities or dimensions necessary for construction. Sometimes even a statue in *lychnites* would have to be composed of two pieces from the start: this is the case with the *Venus de Milo* for example, which is joined at the upper rim of the garment. In Roman times, only the head of a statue might be executed in Parian marble, while the rest would be in another marble. Lesser qualities of Parian marble were quarried much more easily on the surface further up the same valley, but these were less transparent, had a coarser grain and were veined with grey. This quality of marble can be seen in the walls of the Kastro in Parikiá.

The physical characteristics of Parian marble were significant. The transparence was particularly important because the majority of ancient sculpture of the Archaic and Classical periods was coloured—latterly by the application of pigment in a warm wax which penetrated the marble and increased its potential translucence almost two-fold. The artist who coloured a statue was often different from the sculptor: Praxiteles said that he trusted only one person, the painter Nikias, to colour his statues with sufficient sensitivity. The regular, fine-grain, crystalline consistency of the marble was also important, since this meant that it could be polished with emery to an extraordinarily smooth surface. Much of the tactile and formal appeal of the Early Cycladic figurines is owed to this quality.

All marbles handle differently and respond to the artist's tools in a different manner. With a natural monopoly on the finest material, the Parian sculptors were swift to exercise a monopoly on its crafting. There were important schools of sculpture on Paros, and Parian sculptors often travelled with their material to superintend its sculpting at its destination. The greatest sculptures on the Archaic acropolis of Athens and those at Delphi, such as the frieze of the Siphnian Treasury, are in Parian marble. Praxiteles's *Hermes*, as well as his lost, Cnidian *Aphrodite*, the *Venus de Milo*, the *Winged Victory of Samothrace* and the *Nike* of Paionios—are all in the same *lychnites* of Paros, even though each has acquired a different patina with the passage of time and the circumstances of its particular history.

On the hill to the west of the quarries is the heavily fortified and buttressed, 17th century **monastery of Aghios Minás** (dedicated to SS. Minas, Victor and Vincent). It contains a number of *spolia* in its fabric: most important of these is the missing fragment of the relief of the *Nymphs* in the quarries below, which is immured into the solid banister of the steps here.

KOSTOS AND LEFKES

Shortly after Maráthi the road crosses a ridge and turns southwards above a wide and fertile valley sloping down to the west coast, with Naxos visible on the horizon. The attractive villages of **Kostos** (7km) and Léfkes (10.5km) lie below, taking advantage of the relatively abundant water and the hidden position, set back from the coast. They grew rapidly in the 16th century as the population began to concentrate here, fleeing from the coastal scourge of piracy. **Léfkes**, which has the more picturesque setting, was the capital of the island under Turkish rule, up until 1832. It was designed as a walled 'kastro-type' settlement, within a ring of houses forming an enceinte which now defines the centre of the village. The churches often contain *spolia* or have fine 17th century carved portals, such as that of **Aghia Paraskevi**, the village's oldest church which, though rebuilt, was originally a 15th century foundation. Some of the most memorable architecture in the village dates from the turn of the 20th century, such as the neoclassical *Kafeneion*, on the delightful *plateia*, and the '**Priest's House**', a short way to its west, with poly-chrome façade, moulded and coloured niches, *acroteria*, and wrought-iron balcony. Below the *plateia* the church of **Aghios Spyridon** incorporates ancient architectural elements, as does the fountain below it. Aghia Triada, the large church which dominates the village from the east, dates from 1830–35 and contains some of the icons from the three smaller, older chapels which it replaced. The iconostasis and throne in the interior are in local marble.

In the protected valley between Léfkes and Kostos, planted with centuries-old olive groves, the modern road passes a **Byzantine bridge** at a point 500m north of the village: this lies on an ancient route which joined the west coast at Parikiá with the east coast at Marpisa. The stone-paved segment from Léfkes east to Prodromos can be easily followed on foot: the walk takes about 40 minutes. Another pleasant walk is to the **monastery of Aghios Io-annis Kaparou**, immersed in vegetation fed by a spring, in the deep valley directly below the summit of Mt Aghii Pantes, 2.5km southwest of Léfkes.

AROUND MARPISA AND KEFALOS HILL

The east coast of the island is dominated by two uniform conical peaks—Kefalos and Antikéfalos—which rise from the shore with a regular gradient to their summits of c. 170m, like two gateposts framing the sweep of Molos Bay. The area inland is rich in water below the surface and there are several settlements which have their roots in Antiquity. Like Léfkes, the village of **Prodromos** (14.5km) is built as a small, mediaeval *kastro*, with a web of typically Cycladic streets within. The centre can only be reached through one of a series of gates or small tunnels, the eastern one of which is crowned by a belfry, shared by the two 17th century chapels to either side. The village's former name of '*Dragoulás*' comes from the sanctuary of Apollo *Tragios*, who must have preceded Aghios Ioannis Prodromos as protector of the area. In the village 500m to the east of Prodromos, there are quantities of marble elements and *spolia* from some large pagan sanctuary— so many that the village has taken the name '**Mármara**' (15.5km), or 'marbles'. There are column drums built into the houses and into the walls of both the central churches of the village—**Aghios Savvás**, which has a fine example of the local kind of intricate stone belfry, and the church of the **Panaghia Septemvrianí**, or 'Panaghia Pera'. The

doorstep of the latter is made from an ancient boundary marker, which bears the clear inscription '*Η ΟΡΟΣ
ΤΟ ΙΕΡΟ*', 'boundary of the sanctuary' at the right-hand
end. The village water fountain and well-house, a little
way to the north, is ringed by a series of massive marble,
column-drums, which have been given a concave upper
surface so as to act as basins. These must have belonged
to a large Doric temple of the Classical period.

On the lane running due south between Mármara and
Márpisa (16km) is the small fortified **monastery of the
Pantocrator**, with the turreted, four-square appearance
of the Venetian *pyrgi* that are found on Naxos. Tightly fit-
ted into the interior space is the domed *catholicon* and
the abandoned cells. From the cemetery of Márpisa, a
track leads up to the **monastery of Aghios Antonios** on
the summit of **Kephalos Hill** (*open July & Aug 9–1, 5–8;
otherwise the key needs to be obtained from the pappás in
Prodromos*).

The present 16th century monastery buildings, dedicated to
St Anthony the Hermit, are built on the ruins of an earlier,
14th century Frankish church. This stood at the heart of the
fortifications which were begun in the same period by the
Sommaripa Dukes of Paros and Andros. The castle was later
enlarged considerably by Nicolo Sommaripa in c. 1500, who

moved his headquarters here from Parikiá. This process of enlargement can be seen in the **three enceintes** which originally girded the hill, but which are now difficult to perceive in places: the first is passed through by the road, low down on the hill; the second is crossed just below the ruined churches on the southeast side; the third protected the crown of the hill. The last lord of the island, Bernardo Sagredo, held out in this castle against Khaireddin Barbarossa for four days in 1537: he escaped and returned to Venice after the island fell to the Turks. The two **ruined chapels** just below the summit which incorporate several pieces of ancient masonry date from the turn of the 15th century.

The monastery itself and its courtyard contain many ancient capitals, columns, and other architectural elements, suggesting that the site may formerly have been occupied by a pagan sanctuary in the Archaic and Classical period. Certainly, the site is a natural gift both for prehistoric settlement and for later cult. The *catholicon* has a three-aisled, inscribed-cross plan, with two domes. The interior still conserves large areas of 17th century **wall-paintings**, in a style similar to those by the 'Sakellarios Mostratos' in Aghios Ioannis Theologos in Náousa. The most striking element of the interior is the pulpit, which is supported by a slender marble column standing on an upturned, **Ionic capital of Archaic design**. In the sanctuary are marble **escutcheons** of the Sommaripa and other Venetian families, and an elaborate 18th century *ciborium*.

The two chapels below the summit of Kefalos are among the earlier surviving churches on the island. One of the earliest of all, stands just above the shore to the north of **Piso Livadi** (17.5), directly to the south of the hill. The simple, vaulted church of **Aghios Giorgios Thalassitis**, in un-plastered stone, dates from the 13th century, and contains some fine icons. Its walls incorporate marble elements from an Early Christian building.

THE SOUTH AND SOUTHWEST OF THE ISLAND

The south of the island was widely populated in the 3rd and 2nd millennia BC, as the Early Cycladic cemeteries (at Galana Krimna, Avysos and Dryos) and the settlement of the same period discovered at Aghios Myron, between Alyki and Farangas Bay, attest. In later historic times, however, this part of the island was less developed than the north and west, although the presence of several long, straight channels cut in the shelf of rock by the shore at **Dryos** (22km), which served to dry-dock or beach barges and boats, suggests that there must have been significant commerce in the immediate area. In the vicinity of Aspro

Chorio, just north of **Glyphá** (24km), there was a sanctuary of Artemis: the magnificent seated, Archaic goddess, now in the Archaeological Museum, was found near here in 1885, as well as a separate inscribed statue-base naming 'Artemis'. There are ancient *spolia* (which may come from the same sanctuary) in the nearby monastery of **Aghios Ioannis Spiliotis** (26km), built into the entrance of a cave, north of Trypití.

The southeast and south coasts, with their succession of **sandy beaches**, remain an area of primarily recreational appeal, centred on the attractive fishing harbour and sandy bay of **Alikí** (11km from Parikiá by direct route). On the return north to Parikiá from here, however, are a couple of curiosities: just east of the airfield, is the idiosyncratic 'Skorpios Folklore Museum'. Venetos Skiadas is an artesan who specialises in creating models of everything Cycladic, from Tiniot dovecotes, via ancient towers and theatres, to the boats both of recent times and of antiquity. The other point of interest is the 'Valley of Butterflies' or **Petaloudes** (5.5km), above the village of Psychopianá, where an abundant spring feeds dense groves of pomegranate, olive, cypress, fig, rose, prunus and citrus trees. This area was part of the estate of the Mavrogenis family whose fine, stone **mansion** with coloured intonaco is visible in the valley. Prominent on the hillside to the south is the **ruined mediaeval tower of Alisafas**. Outside of the month of June, the valley has an abandoned air; but the butterflies—which are in fact Jersey tiger moths—return each year in dwindling numbers to mate in this well-watered ravine. They are the same species as those which congregate in the Petaloudes valley on Rhodes. There is a small admission charge to enter the meandering walks through the area.

One kilometre north of Petaloudes is the **nunnery of Christos tou Dasous** ('of the forest') (4.5km), dedicated to the Transfiguration of Christ (*open to women only, 10–1*). The monastery, which is sometimes referred to as **Aghios Arsenios**, originally belonged to the Mavrogenis family. It has now become a place of pilgrimage because it contains the tomb of St Arsenios, a patron saint of the island. Arsenios, who was born in Ioannina in 1800, returned late in his life to Paros, where he had spent much of his youth, and became the deacon of the nun's convent here. He died in 1877, and was proclaimed a saint in 1967.

ANTIPAROS

Theodore Bent called Antiparos 'a place without a history'—an ironic comment for a man who pioneered, through his excavations on this island, the discovery of what is now called Early Cycladic culture. One of the oldest organised settlements in the Cyclades is on the islet of **Saliagos** just off Antiparos. The islet, which scarcely appears above sea-level, is visible in the strait (behind the islet of Revmatonisi which is in the foreground), 1km to the north of the ferry route between Paros and Antiparos. Like the other islets in the strait it was originally a low rise on the continuum of land which then joined Paros and Antiparos. Some time—probably in the 2nd millennium BC—a massive seismic movement caused the land to sink by 10–12m, and what was formerly a peninsula became the island of Antiparos, and the summit of Saliagos became a reef.

The **Neolithic settlement** on Saliagos, inhabited by a community of sheep-farmers and fishermen of the late 5th-4th millennium BC, was excavated in 1964–65 by the British School at Athens. Stone foundations of buildings, obsidian arrow-heads, stone implements and pottery were found. A marble figurine of the seated, cross-legged, 'fat-lady' type—an image found also on Malta in the same epoch—was unearthed, as well as some clay chalices of fine workmanship, decorated with abstract designs in white. The settlement has many characteristics in common with that at Fteliá on Mykonos, with which its is more or less contemporary.

Strabo refers to Antiparos as *Oliaros*, which according to the lexicographer Stephanus of Byzantium was a Phoenician name, meaning 'wooded mountain'. The old town of **Antiparos**, 400m inland of the waterfront, was built in the 15th century in an unprotected position which left it vulnerable to pirate attack: it was even less naturally defensible than the *chora* of Kimolos, to which it bears many similarities. It relied on its quadrant of walls formed by the high, reinforced exterior of the circuit of dwellings which opened onto the interior space. The single **gate** into the enclosure is still visible, with rectangular marble blocks from an ancient structure forming part of the base to the right: the arch is faced with dressed stones on its inner side, giving it a slightly pointed profile. Ahead of the gate is a flight of steps which leads to a raised area (now a water cistern) which constituted the base of the original central tower which stood here: some of its lower structure and talus are visible. This suggests that there was at least a tower and cluster of dwellings around it before the planned settlement was begun in 1440—the year in which the island was given in marriage dowry by the Sommaripa Duke of Paros to the Venetian, Leonardo Loredan (sitter in the celebrated portrait by Giovanni Bellini, now in the National Gallery in London). Both to build and populate the new *Kastro*, Loredan brought in settlers from the neighbouring islands. His *Kastro* is a simple but effective piece of urban design—beautifully preserved and still inhabited today. The houses are all created on more or less the same plan, with two or three levels, an exterior balcony reached by a flight of stone steps, and cisterns which collect water from the roofs.

The area outside the *Kastro* is all of later date. The principal church of **Aghios Nikolaos**, which bears its founder's inscription over the door, was begun in 1645, which must mark the beginnings of a tentative expansion beyond the confines of the fortifications. The town continued to be prey to pirate raids however, and as late as 1790 was sacked and left with a markedly reduced population.

The north of the island is mostly agricultural, with a central valley of cultivable land—the **Kambos**—3km south of the Chora. To its west are two lovely beaches, Livádi Bay and, more difficult of access, Monastíria Bay: the latter is delightfully set between two steep hills, and watered by a spring behind. The more mountainous south of the island has seen considerable mining activity.

Bent mentions mines of kalamine, operated by the Messrs Swan who assisted him in his excavations: but there were also mineral-ore mines around Mt Prophitis Elias. Some of the buildings and chutes are still visible.

The **Cave of Antiparos** (*open daily 10.45–3.45 in tours; in winter, reduced hours without tours*), to the east of Prophitis Elias, 8.5km from Chora, has been known and admired since antiquity and visited increasingly since the 17th century. Descending steeply to a depth of over 100m, the space is articulated in chambers of increasing size, festooned with a remarkable density of stalactites and stalagmites. The large, slightly unprepossessing stalagmite by the entrance is said to be 45 million years old and the largest known in Europe.

The quantity of names, dates, inscriptions and graffiti carved into the rock, and going back many centuries, is impressive. Earlier visitors record seeing the name of Archilochus inscribed, and a long inscription recording the names of a group of friends who visited in the 'time of the Archon Kriton'; but these are no longer visible. The names of Byron (probably not authentic), Joseph Pitton de Tournefort, King Otto of Greece, and countless other visitors (mostly French and German) of the 18th and 19th centuries are well preserved along with others, often in beautiful calligraphy.

The path enters through an area called the antechamber, and
then begins to descend steeply in a succession of staircases.
At the bottom a branch leads *right* into the 'Royal Hall', and
left into the 'Cathedral': it is at the extremity of the latter
path that most of the interest and the names are to be found.
Ahead of where the path stops is the "altar". It is inscribed
at its base: HIC IPSE CHRISTUS EJUS NATALIE DIE ME-
DIA CELEBRATO, MDCLXXIII', recording how 'on Christmas Day 1673, mass was celebrated' in the cave. The organ-
iser of this mass was the French Ambassador to the Sublime
Porte, Charles Olier, Marquis of Nointel. He had been sent
to Istanbul by Louis XIV to negotiate better trading privi-
leges for the French with the Ottoman Sultan. On his return
he went via Chios, the Cyclades and Egypt, and finally returned from Athens. He was a keen antiquarian, and col-
lected marbles and inscriptions as he travelled. In his retinue
was Jacques Carrey, whose job was to draw the antiquities
along the way—and to whom we owe the vitally important
sketch of the Parthenon Marbles still *in situ*, in their original
configuration on the building, before they were removed by
Lord Elgin. By all accounts the mass held here was an extraordinary occasion, with the cave illuminated with flares,
the altar decked out with liturgical paraphernalia, fireworks
at the entrance at the moment the Host was consecrated,
the sound of musical instruments, and the clearly eccentric

marquis presiding over what must have been a logistically complicated piece of theatre, requiring much planning and forethought. The arrival of such a grand retinue in the half-abandoned Antiparos of the 17th century must have been a source of wonderment to the few local inhabitants.

Continuing further south on the island, a branch to the left leads a further 5km down to the southern tip of the island from the junction at 8.5km from the Chora. The beautiful promontory is covered in dense maquis and indented all the way down by beautiful **bays and beaches: Soros, Sostis** and **Phaneromeni**, where the tiny chapel provides welcome shade under its 'wings'. By continuing west at the junction, you descend to Aghios Giorgios with good views across the water to the island of Despotikó. It was on the slopes of the hill here, facing the sea, that Theodore Bent's excavations of Early Cycladic cemeteries were made in the winters of 1883 and 1884.

JAMES THEODORE BENT

Theodore Bent's account of the Cyclades, island by island, is such a valuable source of information about their people, customs and beliefs, that no later writer or traveller can afford to ignore it. Bent was only 29 when he visited the islands for the first time in 1882; his wife and travelling companion, Mabel, was six years older. In the 1880s the Greek islands were only just beginning to emerge from the poverty and subjugation of the '*Tourkokratia*', and their often primitive quality of life was at its greatest antithesis to the prosperity of the bourgeois London which the Bents inhabited. But it is that fact which makes their visiting of these (then) remote places so courageous, and Bent's writings about them so ground-breaking. Our debt is twofold: first for the meticulous attention he paid to the diversity of costume, song and dance and to the wayward customs and superstitions of the islanders, which many a lesser soul would not have thought worthy of note; second for his practical examination, through excavation, of a prehistoric Cycladic culture which thitherto was unknown. One of Bent's best qualities is that he doesn't see himself as a great 'explorer' or archaeologist or a pillar of the academic world: he is entirely free of the self-obsession which mars the writings of Schliemann and spoils their greatness with ambiguities and, on occasion, falsehoods. Bent had no pretence greater than the unaffected pleasure he takes in the eccentricities of his island hosts and the genuine interest he has in the origins of their island culture. He enjoys the wide Cycladic landscapes, relishes the odour of antiquity he finds everywhere, and is able to be self-ironic about the dreariness of his 'sexton-like kind of life' as he opens successions of prehistoric graves. At times impatience and irritation can get the better of him: such moments were inevitable—especially for someone sleeping on sodden mattresses under leaking roofs in a gelid December, as he and Mabel did in Naxos. Whereas another writer would not have expressed the impatience, the fact that Bent does is a measure of the un-selfregarding honesty of his account.

Commenting on his excavations on Antiparos—about whose importance he is remarkably unassuming—Bent said that he was 'convinced that a further study of this subject under a more vigorous [?rigorous] system of excavation than I was able to bestow on it would result in many interesting facts becoming known about this primitive race of mankind'. He was quite right; but he was too curious and too restless a soul to continue digging doggedly himself in the Cycladic Islands. Africa and Arabia beckoned. 1889 finds the Bents in the Persian Gulf; 1891 in South and East Africa; 1893 in Ethiopia. In 1897 Bent returned from Arabia with a malarial fever; he contracted pneumonia and died in May of that year at the age of 45.

DESPOTIKO

For access to Despotikó see Practical Information, p. 87.

The remains that are being revealed by excavations year
by year at the site of **Mandra*** on Despotikó are some of
the most remarkable in the Cyclades, and well worth the
trouble involved in getting to see them. The site, undis-
turbed by any later building, on an uninhabited island,
between the sea and the hills behind, is wild and beautiful: and what is coming to light is of remarkable quality.

It is not impossible that in prehistory Despotikó was
joined to Antiparos via the islet of Tsimindiri (or Kimitiri) in the channel between. Certainly as recently as the
6th century BC, Tsimindiri and Despotikó were joined by
an isthmus. Confirmation of this has come from the excavations, in which an altar inscribed '*ΗΕΣΤΙΑΣ ΙΣΘΜΙΑΣ*'
or 'To Hestia of the Isthmus' has come to light, suggesting
that the two islands were linked by a spit of land. Strabo
and Pliny both refer to Despotikó as *Prepesinthos*; but
neither mentions a sanctuary on the island.

No temple has yet been found, but the presence of potsherds
bearing the name '*ΑΠΟΛΛ*' would indicate that the buildings so far discovered were part of a sanctuary of Apollo.

They enclose a rectangular area, at the centre of which is a **semicircular base** (? for votive statues) and, to one side, the **altar of Hestia** mentioned above—both clearly visible. The most interesting building, '***Building A***', lies just behind at the southwestern edge of the excavated area. It is constructed in fine, well-preserved Archaic masonry of Parian marble. It has several rooms, and a portion of its north façade was constituted by a colonnade of eight Doric pillars (south end): the marks left by their bases can be seen. Equally well-preserved, but of later, Classical epoch, is the rectangular, paved building (to south) marked by a large stone bath-tub, a system of drains and circular stone rings for supporting water receptacles. This appears to have been a spacious and well-designed **bathroom** or washing area.

The small, early 7th century BC, painted clay **figurine of a female divinity**, now in the museum in Paros (*see p. 28*) was found in Building A. Votive objects of Eastern Aegean, Rhodian, Cypriot and Egyptian origin have been unearthed, including seals in semi-precious stones, bronze and ivory adornments, metal weapons, and an (Egyptian) ostrich eggshell. A marble Archaic, ***perirrhanterion*** (a sacred water stoup), and fragments of Archaic ***kouroi*** have come to light. Interestingly, two lower portions of 6th century BC *kouroi* were found, reused as doorjambs in the later Classical constructions. A great number of architectural elements from an Archaic, Doric temple have been reused in later walls, too. This suggests that the Archaic temple, which was built at the end of the 6th century BC, was destroyed and its fragments used to build a subsequent version. The site appears to have functioned continuously from the 7th century BC into Roman times.

Several Early Cycladic cemeteries were found on Despotikó when Christos Tsoundas, the pioneer of early Greek archaeology, excavated here in 1898. On the islet of **Tsimindiri** (Kimitiri), foundations of large buildings are visible, and both Hellenistic and Roman burials have been located near the shore; while on the island of **Strongyli**, to the southwest of Despotikó, a ruined Byzantine church on the rocks directly above the shore is built with ancient columns and architectural elements in Parian marble. These islands may seem havens of tranquillity today, but their history is marked by the turbulent activity of the pirates who used them as bases for their operations from antiquity until well into the 19th century.

PRACTICAL INFORMATION

844 00 **Paros**: area 196sq. km; perimeter 111km; resident population 12,514; max. altitude 771 m. **Port authority**: 22840 21240. **Travel information**: Erkyna Travel, T. 22840 22654, fax 22656, www.erkynatravel. com. **General information**: www.paros-greece.gr

840 07 **Antiparos**: area 35sq. km; perimeter 49km; resident population 1,010; max. altitude 301m.

ACCESS

By air: Olympic Air operates two 35-minute flights between Athens and **Paros** daily. The airport is 10.5km from Parikiá.

By boat: There are generally two daily car-ferry connections (4hrs 30mins) to **Paros** from Piraeus (most regularly with *Blue Star Ferries*) in the summer, with frequency dropping in the winter. This is augmented in the summer months (late June–late Sept), by up to four high-speed services daily (minimum 3hrs journey), divided equally between the ports of Piraeus and Rafina for Athens. These services provide an average of three onward connections daily to Naxos, Ios and Santorini.

The car ferry from Pounta (7km south of Parikiá) to **Antiparos** makes the 15 minute crossing 23 times a day from 7am till midnight, at half-hourly intervals in the morning and hourly intervals in the afternoon and evening. The depth of water on the route is nowhere greater than 5m.

Boats across to **Despotikó** need to be arranged with the owner of the taverna which stands just above the jetty at Aghios Giorgios. He has a small craft which makes the journey in ten minutes and costs around €20 return: he will pick you up again at a pre-arranged time.

LODGING

Paros has no shortage of smart places to say: but for simplicity and unpretentious comfort, the following can be recommended. The intimate, family-run **Hotel Dina** in the heart of Parikiá, could not be more central, and is inexpensive, comfortable and quiet (*T. 22840 21325, fax 23525, www.hoteldina.com*). On the edge of Náousa, **Yades Studios** provide tasteful accommodation with helpful management (*T./fax 22840 51072, www.yades. gr*). Beautifully appointed, and with full facilities, is the excellent **Hotel Petres** (*T. 22840 52467, fax 52759, www.petres.gr; open Easter–mid-Oct*). The hotel is set back in the hinterland to the south of Náousa, but with beautiful views north over Plastiras Bay.

Antiparos has a very wide choice of hotels. The **Hotel Artemis** (*T. 22840 61469, fax 61472, www. artemisantiparos.com*) on the north side of the bay, is simple and welcoming; further out is the **Kouros Village** with less character but a better range of services (*T. 22840 61084, fax 61497, www.kouros-village.gr*). For visiting Despotikó, **Oliaros Studios** at Aghios Giorgios, at the southern end of the island, is a delightful alternative (*T./fax 22840 25304/5, www.oliaros.gr*).

EATING

On Paros**, *Levantis**, on Agora Street in Parikiá, is one of the best places to eat in the Cyclades, for food that is refined and yet still Greek: the setting is simple and unpretentious, the cuisine sophisticated and delicious, and the service attentive and pleasant. More expensive and with a refined menu which offers nonetheless some excellent dishes, is **Daphne** in Grávari Street. Amongst the myriad eateries around the three harbours of Náousa, the easternmost taverna on the north shore, **Glafkos**, has excellent seafood and welcoming service. **Le Sud** is also good for more varied and sophisticated cuisine. In Léfkes, **'I Pezoula tis Lichoudias'**, is tiny, and undoubtedly a little artificial, but some of the home-made Greek dishes are nonetheless traditional and of local inspiration.

In Antiparos, locals eat at the **Mezedopoleion 'Tsipouradiko'** by the harbour which has a range of salads and freshly caught seafood.

FURTHER READING

Thomas Hope's *Anastasius, or Memoirs of a Greek*, first published in 1819, is partly based on Nicholas Mavrogenis (*see p. 34–35*) of Paros and his world and times. The book caused a sensation when it was first published in London; By-ron privately admitted that he wished he had been its author. A paperback edition was reissued in 2001, by Elibron Classics. *Paros: History, Monuments etc.* by Yannos Kourayos (Athens 2004) is an exemplary guide to the island's antiquities—clear, authoritative and to the point.

For the remarkable figure of the Marquis de Nointel and his Christmas mass in the Cave of Antiparos, see: Henri Omont, *Relation de la visite du Marquis de Nointel à la grotte d'Antiparos (1673), Bulletin de géographie historique et descriptive*, 1892 (4), pp. 4–33, and Albert Vandal, *L'Odyssée d'un ambassadeur. Les voyages du Marquis de*

Nointel (1670–1680), Paris, 1900. Theodore Bent, *The Cyclades, or Life among the Insular Greeks* (1885), reissued 2002 by Archaeopress, Oxford in the '3rd Guides' series, contains his descriptions of making the earliest excavations of prehistoric Cycladic remains on Antiparos.

INDEX

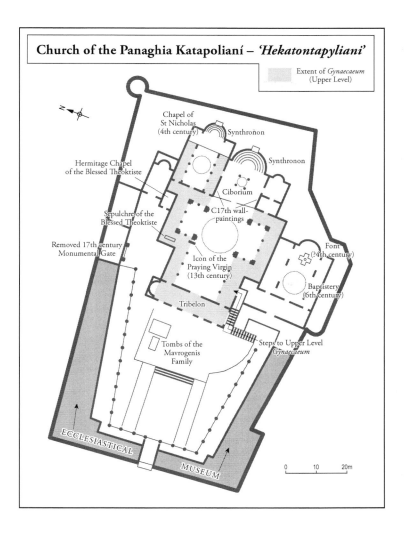

Nigel McGilchrist is an art historian who has lived in the Mediterranean—Italy, Greece and Turkey—for over 30 years, working for a period for the Italian Ministry of Arts and then for six years as Director of the Anglo-Italian Institute in Rome. He has taught at the University of Rome, for the University of Massachusetts, and was for seven years Dean of European Studies for a consortium of American universities. He lectures widely in art and archaeology at museums and institutions in Europe and the United States, and lives near Orvieto.